CAN YOU FIND MY LOVE?™

MORNING

JAN MARQUART

www.CanYouFindMyLove.com

ISBN: 0996854193
ISBN-13: 9780996854191

Cover and Interior by Publish Pros
www.publishpros.com

Books currently available in the "Can You Find My Love?" Series

Other Books by Jan Marquart

FOR ADULTS

Write to Heal

The Mindful Writer, Still the Mind, Free the Pen

The Basket Weaver, a Novel

Kate's Way, a Novel

Echoes from the Womb, a Book for Daughters

Voices from the Land

The Breath of Dawn, a Journey of Everyday Blessings

How to Write From Your Heart (booklet)

How to Write Your Own Memoir (booklet)

A Manual on How to Deal With a Bully in the Workplace

Cracked Open, a Book of Poems

A Writer's Wisdom

To:

_____

NAME

My appreciation to Rich Carnahan, who worked
tirelessly editing the details and photos for this book.
And to master Aiden, who gave valuable reactions to this book,
I send love and hugs. Thank you!

CAN YOU FIND MY LOVE?
is dedicated to all children.

May each child be filled
with love and the fun for learning.

You have received this book
because someone loves you.

Look closely—you will find love hidden
in everyday things that you might
normally take for granted.

This is what it looks like.

When you find the love I have placed
for you, I hope that it warms your
heart and lets you know how
very special you are.

Morning is the START of a new day.

MORNING

WAKE UP

The sun is up, and it's time
for a whole new day to begin.

STRETCh

Stretch out those muscles
and get ready for another great day.

CAN YOU FIND MY LOVE?

RUB YOUR EYES

Clean the "sleep" from the corners of your
eyes and hop out of bed.

CAN YOU FIND MY LOVE?

OPEN YOUR CURTAINS

Morning sunlight lets your body and brain
know that it's time they start working.

CAN YOU FIND MY LOVE?

TURN OFF YOUR NIGHT-LIGHT

Thanks to the sun's rays, there's no longer
the need for the added light.

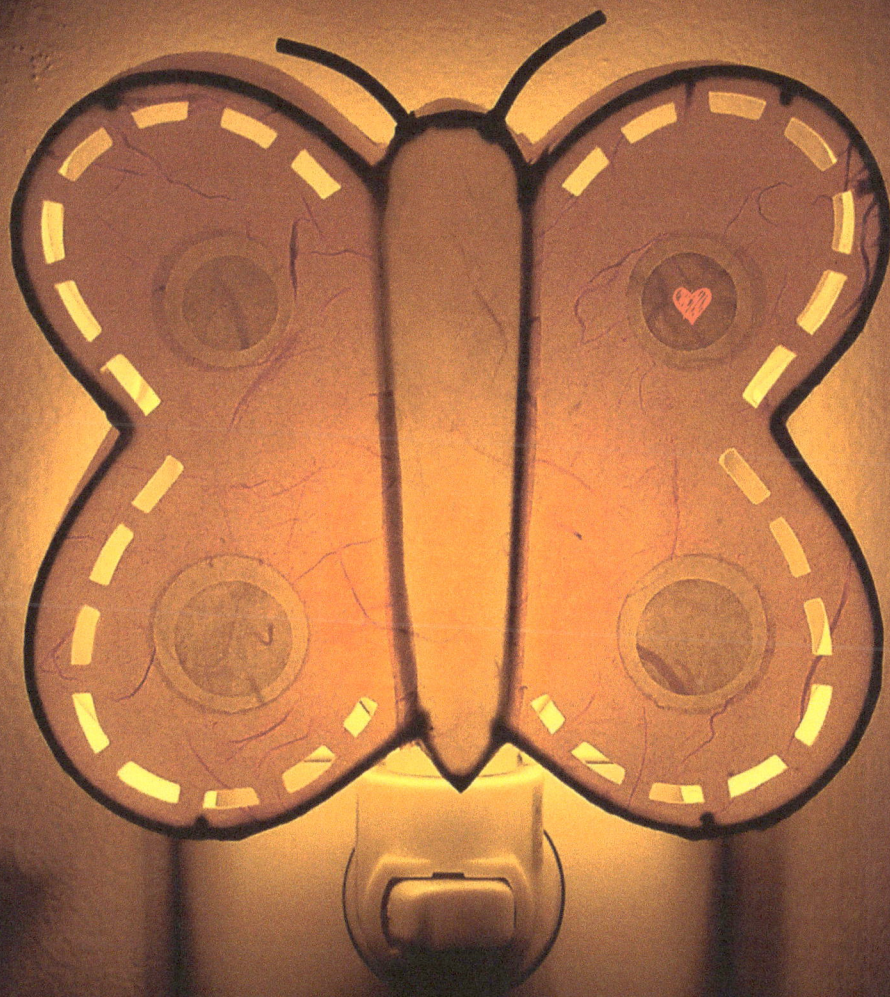

MAKE YOUR BED

Pull up your sheets and finish
your first task of the day.

CAN YOU FIND MY LOVE?

GO TO THE BATHROOM

Going to the toilet makes
your body clean inside.

CAN YOU FIND MY LOVE?

15

GET WASHED

Getting a bath or shower lets you start the new day with clean skin and hair.

GET DRESSED

Putting on clean clothes each day
helps you look and smell good.

PUT ON YOUR SHOES

Shoes protect your feet when
you run and play outside.

BRUSh YOUR hAIR

Brushing your hair keeps it tangle free
and your scalp healthy.

BRUSH YOUR TEETH

Brushing your teeth with a toothbrush and paste will keep them strong.

CAN YOU FIND MY LOVE?

EAT BREAKFAST

Breakfast is the most important meal of the day because it helps you think better.

PICK UP YOUR TOYS

Put your toys away from yesterday
to make room to play some more today.

WALK TO SCHOOL

You'll get exercise and fresh air
when you walk to school.

CAN YOU FIND MY LOVE?

RIDE THE BUS

You can ride with classmates on a bus
when you live too far away to walk.

SAY 'GOOD MORNING'

Be cheerful and smile when you tell others to have a good day.

SLEEP IN

After a hard week, it's nice to get
the time for a few extra hours of sleep.

GO OUTSIDE TO PLAY

Weekend mornings give you time
to exercise and have fun with friends.

WALK THE DOG

Dogs need to use the bathroom in the mornings too and love to be walked.

hAVE A GREAT DAY!

Every day is a brand new day.
Make each one great!

CAN YOU FIND MY LOVE?

43

Did you look close enough
to find all my love?

Can you **DRAW** a few other things you do it the **MORNING**?

Can you **DRAW** a few other things you do it the **MORNING**?

Can you **DRAW** a few other things you do it the **MORNING**?

From:

paste
photo
here

_____

NAME

About the Author

Jan Marquart is a psychotherapist and author. She has published 11 books for adults and has had articles, stories, poems and essays published in various newspapers, journals and magazines across the United States, Australia and Europe. She teaches writing for those over fifty and has taught a dozen writing workshops for Story Circle Network.

Jan has designed a 6-week writing course titled *Unveil the Wounded Self - Write to Heal* which focuses on healing PTSD and has also designed a 6-week writing course titled *The Provocation of Journal Writing* to encourage everyone to write their personal stories. She has written over 100 daily journals.

Jan can be contacted at JanMarquart.com, JanMarquartlcsw.wordpress.com and at her personal email address, jan@canyoufindmylove.com.

Her books can be purchased from all major online book retailers.

www.ingramcontent.com/pod-product-compliance
Lightning Source LLC
Chambersburg PA
CBHW040248100426
42811CB00011B/1189